Lerner SPORTS

MICHAEL JORDAN
FLYING HIGH

JOE LEVIT

LERNER PUBLICATIONS ◆ MINNEAPOLIS

Copyright © 2021 by Lerner Publishing Group, Inc.

All rights reserved. International copyright secured. No part of this book may be reproduced, stored in a retrieval system, or transmitted in any form or by any means—electronic, mechanical, photocopying, recording, or otherwise—without the prior written permission of Lerner Publishing Group, Inc., except for the inclusion of brief quotations in an acknowledged review.

Lerner Publications Company
An imprint of Lerner Publishing Group, Inc.
241 First Avenue North
Minneapolis, MN 55401 USA

For reading levels and more information, look up this title at www.lernerbooks.com.

Main body text set in Myriad Pro Semibold.
Typeface provided by Adobe.

Designer: Susan Fienhage

Library of Congress Cataloging-in-Publication Data

Names: Levit, Joseph, author.
Title: Michael Jordan : flying high / Joe Levit.
Description: Minneapolis : Lerner Publications, [2021] | Series: Epic sports bios (Lerner sports) | Includes bibliographical references and index. | Audience: Ages 7–11 | Audience: Grades K–1 | Summary: "The Chicago Bulls drafted Michael Jordan without knowing he would raise the standard for how basketball is played forever. In this epic biography, learn what makes him a living legend"— Provided by publisher.
Identifiers: LCCN 2019046343 (print) | LCCN 2019046344 (ebook) | ISBN 9781541597433 (library binding) | ISBN 9781728413402 (paperback) | ISBN 9781728400099 (ebook)
Subjects: LCSH: Jordan, Michael, 1963- —Juvenile literature. | Basketball players—United States—Biography—Juvenile literature. | Chicago Bulls (Basketball team)—History—Juvenile literature.
Classification: LCC GV884.J67 L48 2021 (print) | LCC GV884.J67 (ebook) | DDC 796.323092/2 [B]—dc23

LC record available at https://lccn.loc.gov/2019046343
LC ebook record available at https://lccn.loc.gov/2019046344

Manufactured in the United States of America
1-47847-48287-2/6/2020

CONTENTS

NO STOPPING HIM

On June 11, 1997, Michael Jordan and the Chicago Bulls showed up in Salt Lake City, Utah. The Bulls were facing the Utah Jazz in Game 5 of the NBA Finals. The series was tied 2–2. This was an important game, and the Bulls had a wounded warrior on their side. Jordan had a fever of over 100°F (38°C).

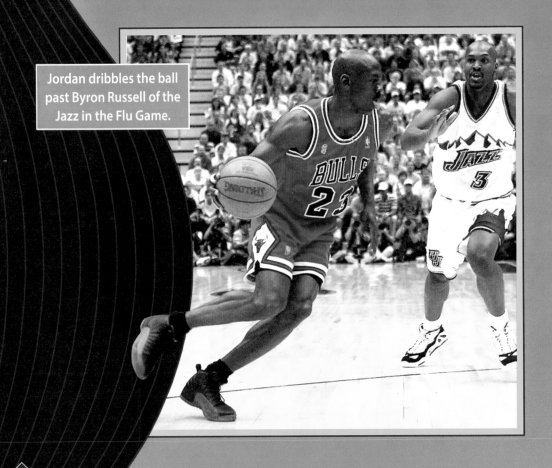

Jordan dribbles the ball past Byron Russell of the Jazz in the Flu Game.

FACTS AT A GLANCE

Date of birth: February 17, 1963

Position: shooting guard and small forward

League: National Basketball Association (NBA)

Professional highlights: hit the game-winning shot in the 1982 National Collegiate Athletic Association (NCAA) Championship Game; third overall pick by the Bulls in the 1984 NBA Draft; won six NBA championships; won 10 NBA scoring titles

Personal highlights: played in statewide and countrywide basketball camps as a teenager; took a break to play baseball for a year during his basketball career; became part owner of the Washington Wizards after his retirement; presented with the Presidential Medal of Freedom in 2016 by President Barack Obama

Jordan celebrates the 1997 NBA championship with the Larry O'Brien Trophy.

The Jazz jumped out to a 16-point lead in the first quarter. By halftime, Jordan had scored 17 points. But he struggled in the third quarter. In the last quarter, Jordan scored seven points in a 10–0 run by the Bulls.

Jordan finished the game with a three-point shot to win with less than a minute left. He was partly carried off the court, later revealing that he almost fainted. For many people, it proved that Jordan was a legend in the making.

GROWING UP

Michael Jordan was born in Brooklyn, New York, but he grew up with four siblings in North Carolina. His parents set solid ground rules to keep their children out of trouble and in school.

Michael with his parents James and Deloris Jordan in their home.

Long before Michael would compete against the best basketball players in the world, he played against his older brother. Larry was shorter and a year older than Michael, but he was just as competitive and athletic. Every day, the two would battle until bedtime on a basketball court

Michael only began defeating his older brother, Larry, after outgrowing him in high school.

SIBLING RIVALRY

Michael's high school basketball coach, Pop Herring, compared him to his brother. "Larry was so driven and so competitive an athlete that if he had been 6'2" [1.9 m] instead of 5'7" [1.7 m], I'm sure Michael would have been known as Larry's brother instead of Larry always being known as Michael's brother."

that their father, James, had built in their backyard. In time, Michael outgrew his big brother and began to win consistently, but that didn't set him up for instant success.

As a sophomore in high school, Michael tried out for the varsity basketball team. The team had already filled 14 of the 15 slots with players from the previous year. That meant only one slot was open. Michael's friend, Leroy Smith, made the team instead. Michael pushed himself and joined the junior varsity team. He soon became a leader, and the next year he was a star on the varsity team.

After seeing Michael play, Coach Dean Smith recruited him to play for the University of North Carolina.

The summer before his senior year, Michael was invited to a statewide basketball camp. The camp was run by Dean Smith. Smith was head coach of the University of North Carolina men's basketball team, the Tar Heels. Michael did so well that Smith's assistant head coach, Roy Williams, told another assistant, "I think I just saw the best 6'4" [1.9 m] high school player I've ever seen."

Williams arranged for Michael to play in a Five-Star camp, one of the best for young athletes. He thrived against players from across the country. Colleges everywhere wanted to recruit him. Fortunately for the Tar Heels, Michael's parents felt Williams and Smith would be a good influence on their son. He signed to play for them.

Michael's older brother wore jersey number 45. When Michael chose his number at North Carolina, he took half of his brother's number and rounded it up to 23.

Jordan makes the winning basket against the Georgetown Hoyas during the 1982 NCAA Finals.

The Tar Heels made it to the National Collegiate Athletic Association (NCAA) Finals in 1982. They were going up against the powerhouse Georgetown Hoyas. The Hoyas were led by future NBA Hall of Famer Patrick Ewing.

With 17 seconds left in the game, Jordan hit the game-winning jump shot that would change his life forever. "Before that, I was Mike Jordan," he reflected. "All of a sudden I make that shot and I'm Michael Jordan."

ON THE RISE

Jordan won the NCAA College Player of the Year award in 1984. Later that year, he was drafted with the third overall pick by the Chicago Bulls. Chosen ahead of him were two centers, Hakeem Olajuwon and Sam Bowie. Olajuwon would make the Hall of Fame. Bowie, however, had a

Shortly after the 1982 NCAA Finals, Jordan was featured on the cover of the *Sporting News* magazine, a national sports journal.

The Sporting News

PRICE: $1.50

rop: TSN's All-America Team

eview: Linemen, Tight Ends

Braxton Settle Their Debate

PLAYER OF THE YEAR
North Carolina's
Michael Jordan

NORTH
23
CAROLI

SPALD

forgettable career. He later admitted that he lied about a leg injury before the draft because he hoped to get picked before Jordan.

Jordan's outgoing personality and athletic abilities made him a star. Companies such as Gatorade and Wheaties hired him to help endorse their products. Jordan went on to become Rookie of the Year and was chosen to play in the 1984 All-Star Game. But in Jordan's first five seasons, the Bulls won only three playoff series. The rise of the Detroit Pistons prevented the Bulls from finding success early on.

IF THE SHOE FITS

Initially, Jordan wanted to sign an endorsement deal with Adidas. But the company only wanted to sign players who were over 7 feet (2.1 m) tall. Nike swooped in to sign Jordan instead. Together, they began to dominate the athletic shoe market.

The Bad Boys slowed Jordan down for several seasons, but he only got better and better.

The Detroit Pistons' aggressive style on the court had earned them the nickname Bad Boys. To keep up with Jordan, the team came up with the Jordan Rules: they would play an aggressive mental and physical game, shoving and taunting Jordan whenever possible. The goal was to make sure Jordan didn't drive the lane for easy layups or excite the crowd with dunks. "It was important that we mentally intimidated him," said Pistons center Bill

The Bad Boys often swarmed Jordan, giving him little time to think and little space to move.

Laimbeer. "Whether we had to knock him down or send three guys at him, or just look mean, ugly nasty in his face."

The Pistons knocked the Bulls out of the playoffs for three straight seasons, from 1988 to 1990. In both 1989 and 1990, the Pistons beat the Bulls in the Conference Finals and went on to win the NBA championship.

DAYS OF THE DYNASTY

In 1989, the Bulls hired Phil Jackson as head coach. Jackson and team assistant Tex Winter created the triangle offense. It required Jordan to pass the ball to his teammates when he was too well guarded. Jordan had a hard time trusting his teammates to knock down big

Jackson coached the Bulls for nine years, taking them to six NBA championships with Jordan leading the way.

Jordan looks for a pass while guarded by LaBradford Smith of the Washington Bullets in 1991.

shots. Eventually, Jordan began passing the ball, and the Bulls quickly improved. The triangle offense proved itself when the Bulls finally topped the Pistons 4–0 in the 1991 Conference Finals.

Jordan was a star in the NBA Finals. The Bulls won the 1991 series against the LA Lakers 4–1. Confident and experienced, the Bulls repeated as NBA champions in 1992.

The 1992 US Men's Basketball team did not lose a single game. They would be remembered as the Dream Team.

Jordan was a man on a mission. He wanted to help the Bulls win yet another NBA championship, something that had never happened before. The feat, which became known as a three-peat, occurred when the Bulls took out the Phoenix Suns 4–2 in the 1993 Finals.

The 1992 US Olympics basketball lineup was filled with NBA superstars, including Jordan. *Sports Illustrated* called them the Dream Team. They beat other teams easily and crushed Croatia 117–85 for the gold medal.

RETIRING AND RECHARGING

Jordan was the ultimate competitor. He had a difficult time turning off this side of him when off the court. His father once admitted, "What he does have is a

Jordan's desire to compete wasn't something he hid from the public. He often showed his enthusiasm for winning.

competition problem. He was born with that . . . the person he tries to outdo most of the time is himself."

In July 1993, Jordan's father was murdered. Jordan made the decision to retire from basketball. He always loved baseball and turned to the sport during his time of distress. He joined a Chicago White Sox minor-league team in 1994.

In baseball, Jordan was finally able to take the jersey number he'd always wanted, number 45.

Jordan didn't have enough baseball experience to compete with players in the minor leagues.

CARD SHARK

While on a visit to teammate Buzz Peterson's family during his North Carolina days, Peterson caught Jordan cheating while playing a game of Go Fish. Peterson was stunned. He couldn't believe that Jordan wanted to win so badly that he'd cheat during a friendly card game!

Jordan didn't perform as he'd hoped to, but his time away from basketball renewed his love for it. "Those minor leaguers were the best thing that happened to me," said Jordan. "It was their true love for the game. And I lost that, and I found it again playing minor league baseball."

Jordan returned to the Bulls partway through the 1995 season. Though he helped them make the playoffs, they exited the tournament early. The next three years would make NBA history yet again. Jordan was back and he made sure everyone knew it. The Bulls secured another three-peat from 1996 to 1998.

Before Jordan officially announced his return to the NBA, fans were waiting and ready for him.

Jordan is presented the NBA MVP Award by commissioner David Stern on May 21, 1996.

BEYOND THE BULLS

At 35 years old, Jordan announced his second retirement from the NBA. About a year later, in 2000, he became part owner and general manager of the Washington Wizards. He reentered the game and played for the Wizards for three years. In 2003, he became the first 40-year-old player to score 43 or more points in a game.

In the three years Jordan played for the Wizards, it was clear his physical abilities were not what they used to be.

Since retirement, Jordan has grown his Jordan Brand of athletic gear.

Jordan retired for the third and final time in April 2003. He purchased part of the Charlotte Bobcats (later renamed the Charlotte Hornets) and continued to grow his Jordan Brand. He became one of the richest people in America.

SIGNIFICANT CAREER STATS

Ranks first in NBA history with 30.12 career points per game

Ranks third in NBA history with 2,514 career steals

Won the regular-season MVP Award five times

Won the Finals MVP Award six times

Selected All-Defensive First Team nine times

Won the NBA scoring title 10 times (the most all-time wins)

GLOSSARY

All-Defensive First Team: one of the best defensive players in the NBA, according to votes by sports media members

endorsement: a payment made to a player by a company whose product the player will promote

intimidate: to scare or bully

jump shot: a shot made by jumping into the air and releasing the ball with one or both hands at the peak of the jump

lane: the painted area under the basket where players can take closer shots

layup: a player uses one hand to bounce the ball off the backboard and into the basket

recruit: find and add basketball players to a team

run: when one team scores a lot of points in a row without the other team scoring any

three-peat: winning three NBA titles in a row

SOURCE NOTES

9   Tim Ott, "Michael Jordan's Life before He Became an NBA Star," Biography, last modified June 24, 2019, https://www .biography.com/news/michael-jordan-life-before-nba-early -career.

10   "Michael Jordan—ESPN Basketball Documentary," YouTube video, 42:44, posted by AllBasketballUniverse, October 13, 2013, 12:38, https://www.youtube.com/watch?v=nFK_q4sw YNs&t=1563s.

12   Scott Rafferty, "Flashback: Michael Jordan Begins Legendary Rise with Game-Winning NCAA Championship Shot," *Rolling Stone*, March 29, 2017, https://www.rollingstone.com/culture /culture-sports/flashback-michael-jordan-begins-legendary -rise-with-game-winning-ncaa-championship-shot-111612/.

15–16   "Michael Jordan Documentary," 23:21.

20–21   "Michael Jordan," Biography, last modified October 22, 2019, https://www.biography.com/athlete/michael-jordan.

23   "Michael Jordan Documentary," 32:45.

FURTHER INFORMATION

Editors of *Sports Illustrated Kids. Big Book of Who, Basketball: The 101 Stars Every Fan Needs to Know.* New York: Time Books, 2015.

Kramer, Sydelle. *Basketball's Greatest Players.* New York: Random House, 2015.

Mason, Tyler. *Michael Jordan and the Chicago Bulls.* Minneapolis: SportsZone, 2019.

Michael Jordan Stats
https://www.basketball-reference.com/players/j/jordami01.html

Monson, James. *Behind the Scenes Basketball.* Minneapolis: Lerner Publications, 2020.

NBA.com
https://www.nba.com/

INDEX

PHOTO ACKNOWLEDGMENTS

Image credits: Jeff Haynes/AFP/Getty Images, pp. 4, 6; Pongnathee Kluaythong/EyeEm/
Getty Images, pp. 5, 28; Buck Miller/The LIFE Images Collection/Getty Images, p. 7;
Dimitrios Kambouris/WireImage/Getty Images, p. 8; Focus on Sport/Getty Images,
pp. 10, 11, 15, 17, 18, 21; Bettmann/Getty Images, pp. 12, 16; Sporting News/Getty Images,
pp. 13, 25; Dimitri Iundt/Corbis/VCG/Getty Images, p. 19; Vincent Laforet/AFP/Getty
Images, p. 20; Jonathan Daniel/Getty Images, p. 22; Jonathan Daniel/ALLSPORT/Getty
Images, p. 24; Jamie Squire/Getty Images, p. 26; Catherine Steenkeste/Getty Images
Sport/Getty Images, p. 27.

Cover: Vincent Laforet/Getty Images (dunk); Tim DeFrisco/Getty Images (run).